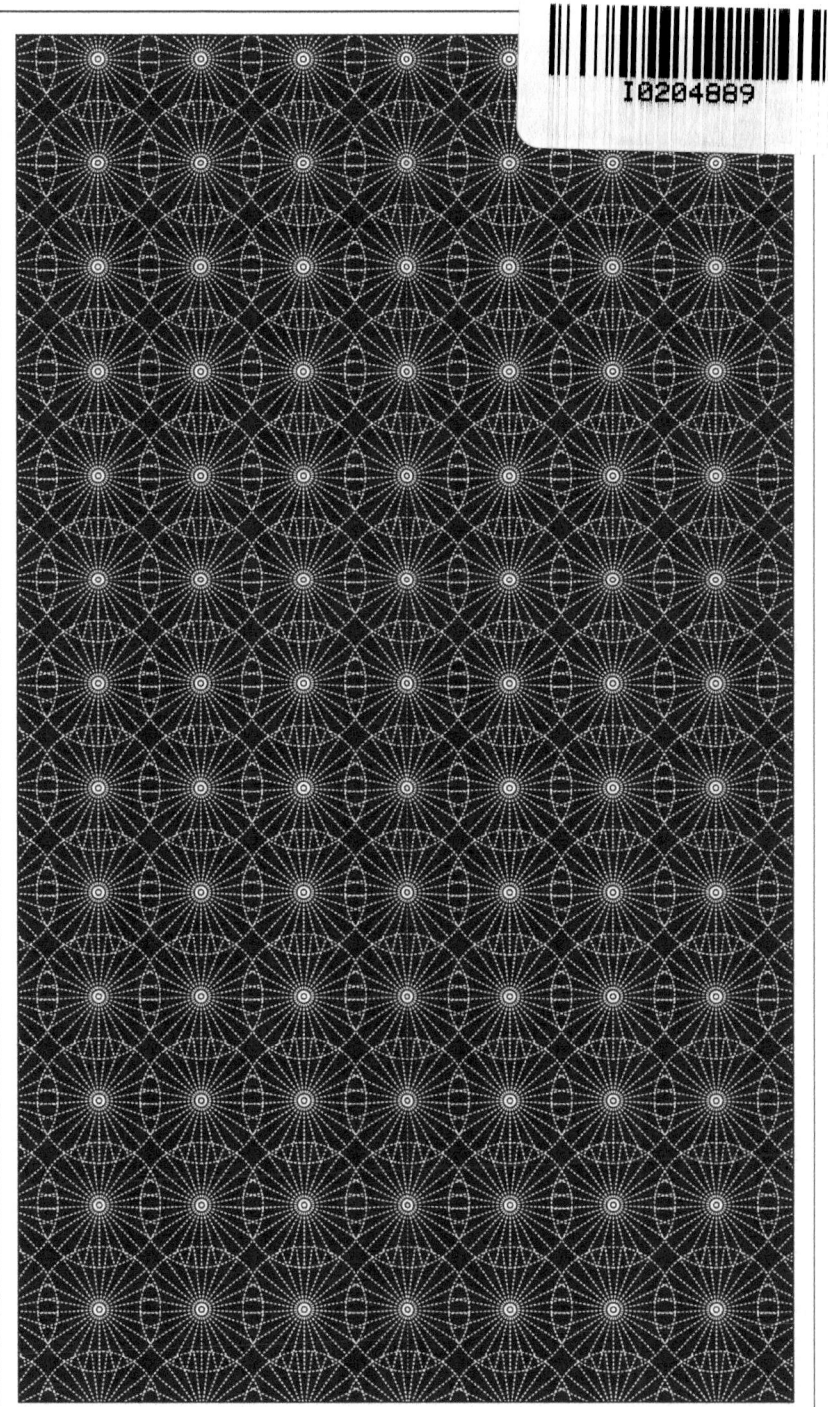

THE INSIDE GAME

MASTERING THE MIND
STRENGTHENING THE SPIRIT
LEADING WITH PURPOSE

Gus "BigDawg" Felder

BIGDAWG
BOOKS
2025

†

THE INSIDE GAME
Gus BIGDAWG Felder
© 2025

ISBN 978-1-952911-68-2
All rights reserved. No part of this book may be
used in the context of another work without
written permission of the author or
BIGDAWG BOOKS
Lincoln, Nebraska

Cover design by Prairie Muse Books Inc.

TABLE OF CONTENTS

Dedication	7
Introduction	9
Why the Inside Game Matters	9
Control the Controllables	11
What are you trying to control right now that isn't yours to manage?	16
Forged in the Fire	19
From Non-Qualifier to Game-Changer	19
What's your current obstacle, and what is it revealing about your character?	23
Lead by Serving	27
Who's depending on you right now, not for answers but for presence?	30
Strength Through Stillness	33
Where do you need to slow down?	37
Know Thyself	41
Who are you really?	45
Brotherhood, Not Just Teammates	49
Stand Tall in the Fire	55
Are you in a fire season right now?	58
The Locker Room Pulpit	61
Where is your pulpit?	64
Fatherhood Is Legacy	67

Table of Contents continued...

One Team, One Vision	**73**
Who are you trying to lead right now, and are you all aiming at the same goal?	76
The Power of Presence	**79**
Where are you rushing through life and missing opportunities to be present?	82
Beyond the Final Whistle	**85**
Build Builders	**91**
Look around you. Who in your circle needs what you've learned the hard way?	94
The Health Equation: Leading From the Inside Out	**97**
What part of your personal health have you been putting on the back burner?	101
Finish With Fire	**105**
See You on the Field	**111**
Acknowledgments	**115**
About the Author	**117**

DEDICATION

To my wife, Kelly

From the moment we met at Red Rock Job Corps, two 16-year-old kids from Philadelphia with big dreams and bigger obstacles, I knew there was something special about you. From the days of me picking on you while in class during our time at Red Rock, to you growing into the lovely, loving mother and mimi you have become. What I didn't know then was how deeply your love, strength, and faith would anchor my life.

Together, we built a foundation not on ease, but on God, His grace, His timing, and His promises. Through every season, the late nights, the lost jobs, the relocations, the hospital visits, the tight budgets, the growing pains, you never wavered. You stood beside me, lifted me, challenged me, and loved me through it all.

We've endured more than many will ever know, but we've also experienced a love many will never find—a love forged through faith, tested by life, and strengthened by time.

You are the heart of our home, the keeper of our children's peace, and the quiet hero behind every chapter of this story. I've seen you sacrifice without complaint, raise our family with grace, and love me through both my calling and my flaws.

This book, this legacy, this life we've built, none of it happens without you.

I love you endlessly.

Thank you for walking with me every step of the way.

Forever your husband,
Gus "BigDawg" Felder

8

INTRODUCTION

Why the Inside Game Matters

The world will judge you by what it sees on the outside: your title, your status, your résumé, your wins and losses. But real leadership…real strength…real success? That starts on the **inside**.

I've been a player, a coach, a teacher, a husband, a father, a mentor, and in every season of my life, I've learned that external achievements mean very little if the internal foundation is broken. *The inside game*—your character, your mindset, your spiritual core—is what determines how you respond when life hits hard, when people walk away, when plans fall apart, and when God calls you higher.

I wasn't supposed to make it. I was a high school dropout raised in North Philadelphia, a product of a broken system and hardened streets. But God had a different plan. Through His grace, I found redemption, discipline, education, and purpose. I made it to Penn State. I earned three degrees. I played in the NFL. I coached at the highest levels. But more than anything, I built a life based on **faith, consistency, and service**.

This book isn't about me, it's about what I've learned from the mountains and the valleys. It's a blueprint for how to lead, grow, and endure from the inside out. Each chapter includes lessons rooted in **Stoic philosophy**, **spiritual devotion**, and **real-life leadership**. You'll hear about the moments that tested me, stretched me, and taught me who I truly am.

If you're reading this, you're likely on your own journey navigating work, family, calling, doubt, and growth. My prayer is that this book becomes a companion on that path. It helps you wrestle with the hard stuff, refocus on what matters, and finish your race with fire.

Because the truth is, it's not the crowd that makes you great. It's not the lights, the titles, or the trophies. It's what happens when no one's watching. **It's the work you do on your heart, your habits, and your hope.**

That's the *Inside Game*. And that's why it matters.

Let's get to it.

Gus "BigDawg" Felder

1

CONTROL THE CONTROLLABLES

Stoic Quote:

"You have power over your mind, not outside events. Realize this, and you will find strength."
MARCUS AURELIUS

LONG BEFORE I EVER "DROPPED OUT," I was already slipping.

I entered **Murrell Dobbins Tech** on North 22nd Street, hoping a trade program would be my ticket out of North Philly. But by the end of my freshman year, my attendance record looked like a pair of ripped sneakers with holes everywhere. I'd skip first and second period, drift through the halls, and post up on the corner with friends who carried more hurt than homework. Teachers called my name every morning; most mornings, the answer was silence.

When I dropped out of high school in Philadelphia, I felt like a statistic. One of the thousands slipping through the cracks of a system that was broken long before I walked its halls. The Philadelphia public school system wasn't built for kids like me to succeed; it was underfunded, overcrowded, and overwhelmed. Some days, just surviving the day felt like the only win available.

There was no dramatic exit. I didn't flip a desk or shout in protest. I just stopped showing up. And for a time, no one really noticed.

That could've been the end of my story, and for a lot of people around me, it was. But there was something still burning inside me. Maybe it was the words of my mother, Barbara Ann Felder, echoing in my mind, or maybe it was God's whisper that said, *"You're not done yet."*

That could've been the final chapter, but God had another paragraph.

Eventually, I enrolled in **Red Rock Job Corps.** The **Red Rock Job Corps Center** is a **free, residential vocational training school** located in **Colley Township (Lopez), Sullivan County, Pennsylvania**, on Red Rock Mountain within the boundaries of **Ricketts Glen State Park.** I showed up not as a scholar, but as someone desperate for a fresh start. It didn't hand me a miracle. What it gave me was structure, discipline, and an opportunity for a clean slate. I began learning the **carpentry trade**, and somewhere between the hammer and the nails, something deeper was being built: my self-worth.

But the most important thing I found at Job Corps wasn't a trade, it was **my wife, Kelly**. We met at Red Rock, two young people trying to rewrite our futures. Neither of us imagined then that we'd spend the next **30 years together**, raising a family and building a life grounded in faith, commitment, and purpose.

Something else awakened in me at Job Corps: **a new love for education**. I didn't want my last chapter to be a dropout. I wanted more. After completing my carpentry certification, I made the decision to go back to high school. That decision changed everything. Job Corps also ignited something I thought had died back at Dobbins and Simon Gratz: a hunger to learn.

I re-enrolled at **Berwick Area High School**, three hours from Philly but worlds away from the chaos I left behind. What I found there wasn't just a school, it was **a town that loved me into the man I was meant to become**.

Coach **George Curry**, a Pennsylvania coaching legend, handed me a playbook the size of a college textbook and said, *"When you work hard, great things will happen."* He wasn't bluffing. From the moment I stepped into his program, I was treated with high expectations and unwavering belief. He didn't just teach X's and O's; he modeled what manhood, discipline, and accountability looked like—every single day. Coach **Cosmo Curry**, George's son and the school's strength coach, became my mentor and big brother all in one. He helped mold me not just in the weight room, but in life. Whether I needed an extra set of squats or someone to talk to after a rough day, Cosmo was there. He taught me how to lead from the front, how to take care of my body, and how to take ownership of my future.

And then there was **Sallie Johnson**, who took me into her home like I was her own son. Her kindness wasn't flashy; it was steadfast, quiet, and unconditional. She made sure I had what I needed, whether it was a hot meal, a warm bed, or a listening ear. In a town where I started as an outsider, she and so many others made me feel like **family**.

The **teachers at Berwick** didn't see a former dropout; they saw a young man trying to rewrite his story. They challenged me, supported me, and celebrated my small wins like they were state championships. For the first time, I realized that **education wasn't a punishment; it was a key.** The more I showed up in class, the more I saw the connection between the discipline I had in football and the excellence I could achieve academically.

It was in Berwick that I fell in love with learning. The football field gave me confidence, but the classroom gave me **vision**. I started to understand that I could use athletics not just as an escape but as a **bridge** to something bigger. I could build a life. I could lead. I could **give back** one day, just as so many were giving to me.

Two years later, I was **a better student**, a **two-time state champion**, and a young man with a new blueprint for life. That blueprint started with the community of Berwick, a place that proved to me that **faith, family, and education** could coexist with football in powerful ways.

Spiritual Devotion

"Do not conform to the pattern of this world, but be transformed by the renewing of your mind."
Romans 12:2

In the world's eyes, I was behind. I was a dropout, a trade student, a kid with a past. But God doesn't look at timelines. He looks at **hearts in motion**. He transforms from the inside out.

At Red Rock, in the stillness of early mornings or moments of reflection, I began to believe again, not in the system, but in the **God who gives second chances**. Every time I opened my

Bible or prayed quietly before sleep, I felt the roots of something deeper anchoring me.

I was still rough around the edges. But I had a foundation now, and it was solid.

The Leadership Lesson

Leadership starts long before someone calls you "Coach" or "Boss." It begins the moment you decide that your past will not decide your future. It begins when you take ownership of your **thoughts, your habits, and your attitude**.

At Job Corps, I didn't have a platform or a position. What I had was a choice: to take the reins of my own life.

When I stepped onto that high school football field in Berwick, I wasn't just trying to win games. I was proving to myself and to others that your beginnings don't define your ceiling. **Controlling the controllables** meant I could finally stop being a victim of my circumstances and start becoming a vessel of purpose.

The Challenge to the Reader

What are you trying to control right now that isn't yours to manage?

Take a moment. Write it down. Now, list what *is* in your control:

> Your attitude
> Your effort
> Your mindset
> Your willingness to grow

Now pray:

> *"Lord, help me release what's not mine to carry and give me the strength to lead what You've entrusted to me, starting with myself. Amen."*

You don't have to have all the answers. You just have to be willing to take the first step.

Because leadership begins not when others follow you, but when you finally follow what God has placed inside you.

✝

†

†

2

FORGED IN THE FIRE

FROM NON-QUALIFIER TO GAME-CHANGER

Stoic Quote:

*"The impediment to action advances action.
What stands in the way becomes the way."*
MARCUS AURELIUS

WHEN I GOT THE ACCEPTANCE LETTER to Penn State, it should've been one of the proudest moments of my life, a high school dropout from North Philly, now headed to one of the most prestigious football programs in the country. But I wasn't celebrating. The letter came with a label: **NCAA non-qualifier.** That meant I couldn't receive a scholarship right away, couldn't play in games, and couldn't travel with the team.

To the world, I wasn't a student-athlete. I was a maybe. A risk. A longshot.

I was also a soon-to-be newlywed, a new father, and the big brother my family was counting on. I didn't have time to sulk. I had too many mouths to feed and a dream to resurrect. My wife, Kelly, and I had just gotten married. Our daughter, Destiny, was still in diapers. My mother back in Philly asked me to take in my younger brother so he wouldn't get eaten alive by the same school system that almost swallowed me. So now, I wasn't just a student trying to make it, I was a husband, a father, and a protector.

I showed up on campus hungry, not just for food, but for **change**. I created my own routine before dawn with the help of John "JT" Thomas and his strength staff.

I didn't settle for the minimum 2.0 GPA. In fact, I made the **Dean's List two of my first three semesters** and earned my full scholarship by the following summer. But no textbook could prepare me for the pressure of balancing school, football, marriage, and fatherhood. I was writing papers at 2 a.m. with a baby monitor buzzing beside me. I was running to class after dropping off my little brother at his high school.

Coach **Joe Paterno** noticed. He saw the grind, the grades, the grit. He saw me lead not with a title but with action. He pulled me aside one day and said:

"You have a great work ethic, and you are mature beyond your years. This program isn't just building football players; it's building men."

By my junior year, I was starting on the offensive line, going head-to-head with some of the best athletes in the country. But I had already fought bigger battles in the classroom, in my home, in my soul. What people saw on Saturdays was just the surface. What they didn't see was the fire that forged it all.

That experience shaped me more than anything else. It taught me how to **manage pressure, stay focused, and lead without excuses**. The world saw obstacles, I saw opportunity. The road was steep, but it was building something in me that success alone never could.

Spiritual Devotion

"Consider it pure joy, my brothers and sisters, whenever you face trials of many kinds, because you know that the testing of your faith produces perseverance."
James 1:2–3

Penn State not only sharpened my body but also refined my soul. While the outside world saw an athlete striving for success, the more profound truth was this: God was pruning and preparing me.

I didn't become a man of character despite the pressure; I became one because of it. Every early morning, every late-night paper, and every moment I wanted to quit but didn't, that was God at work, building perseverance, endurance, and vision. We often pray for open doors but forget that God uses resistance to build our readiness. That was Penn State for me, a resistance that reshaped my life.

The Leadership Lesson

Leadership doesn't start when you get the title; it begins when you stop making excuses.

It would've been easy to blame the system for labeling me a non-qualifier. To fold under the pressure of college football, academics, marriage, fatherhood, and being a big brother all at once. But I learned that pressure doesn't break leaders, **it forges them**.

Obstacles don't block the path. They **become** the path. And the leaders who rise are the ones who accept the challenge, commit to the grind, and **lead through adversity**, not around it.

The Challenge to the Reader

What's your current obstacle, and what is it revealing about your character?

Write down the one thing that feels like it's standing in your way right now. Then ask:

What strength is this challenge forcing me to develop?

What would it look like to trust that this obstacle might actually be part of God's plan?

Now pray:

> *"God, when the road feels uphill and the weight feels heavy, remind me why I started. Give me the strength to keep showing up, the wisdom to grow through the pressure, and the faith to believe this struggle has purpose. Use this season to shape me, not stop me. Amen."*

Because here's the truth: **the Fire is the path.** Don't run from it. Walk through it. And let it transform you.

†

†

†

†

3

LEAD BY SERVING

Stoic Quote:

"Don't explain your philosophy. Embody it."
Epictetus

LEADERSHIP ISN'T ABOUT BEING SEEN. It's about showing up when no one's watching.

By the time I reached my **senior year at Penn State**, I had already overcome the odds as a former NCAA non-qualifier, earned a full scholarship, and had become a starter under **Coach Joe Paterno**. But I still had one more mountain to climb: graduating in four years to be eligible for a **fifth year**, per NCAA rules at the time.

It was a pressure-cooker season. Coach Paterno agreed to a modified schedule, allowing me to focus on my academics. That meant I worked out **every morning at 5:30 a.m.**, before the campus ever woke up. I was excused from spring football practice not because I was taking a break, but because I was gearing up for something bigger: **a 27-credit summer**.

That summer was one of the hardest seasons of my life. I was a father, a husband, a brother, a leader on the team, and now, a full-time student grinding through an academic load most people couldn't imagine.

But by the grace of God and with a **3.6 GPA**, I did it. I graduated **before fall camp** and earned my fifth year of eligibility.

That year, **2002**, was special. After two losing seasons, Penn State got back on track. We helped **Larry Johnson** rush for over 2,000 yards, becoming only the **fourth running back in NCAA history** to do so at the time. He won nearly every major award except the Heisman. Our team sent multiple players to the **first and second rounds** of the 2003 NFL Draft.

And me? I went **undrafted** and was signed by the **Cleveland Browns** as a free agent. My NFL career was short; I was with the team from **April to November,** but what came next was providential.

Penn State brought me back. I became a **student assistant coach**, learning the game from the other side. I knew the weight room. I knew the locker room. But now I was learning the whiteboard, the strategy, the mentorship. And then came one of the most powerful full-circle moments of my life: I was offered a chance to become the **head football coach at Simon Gratz High School,** the **same school I had dropped out of years before.**

That wasn't just a job. That was redemption. That was God's grace in motion. I didn't go back for the title. I went back to **serve** to be the man I once needed.

Spiritual Devotion

"For even the Son of Man did not come to be served, but to serve, and to give His life as a ransom for many."
Mark 10:45

Jesus led by stooping low by showing up for the hurting, the overlooked, the broken. That's the model I try to follow, not just as a coach, but as a man.

We live in a world that celebrates spotlight leadership, but God honors **servant leadership**. He blesses those who put people over pride and calling over comfort.

My journey taught me this: it's not about who knows your name, it's about **whose lives are better because you showed up.**

The Leadership Lesson

Servant leadership is not a weakness. Its **strength is under submission.**

Real leaders don't need applause. They don't need platforms. They don't lead from ego, they lead from love. From grit. From grace.

Whether I was pushing through a 27-credit summer, walking back into the NFL facility after a cut, or walking into my old high school as a coach, my goal wasn't to impress. It was to **invest**.

If you want to lead others, you first have to lead yourself. And that kind of leadership? It always starts with service.

The Challenge to the Reader

Who's depending on you right now, not for answers but for presence?

Who can you show up for this week without needing credit?

Where can you put people ahead of pride?

What would it look like to **serve where you once struggled**?

Servant leadership changes lives, starting with your own.

Now pray:

> *"Lord, help me lead with humility, not for recognition but for impact. Remind me that greatness is not found in titles, but in how I treat others when no one is watching. Teach me to serve where I once struggled and to lift others with the same grace You've shown me. May my presence speak louder than my words, and may I never forget that leadership starts with love. Amen."*

†

†

†

4

STRENGTH THROUGH STILLNESS

Stoic Quote:

"If you are distressed by anything external, the pain is not due to the thing itself, but to your estimate of it. And this you have the power to revoke at any moment."
MARCUS AURELIUS

THERE'S A KIND OF PRESSURE IN LEADERSHIP that's hard to explain, especially when everything looks like it's going well on the outside. From Simon Gratz High School in North Philadelphia to Cheyney University and Melbourne High School in Florida, I wore many hats: **head coach, strength coach, offensive coordinator, father, husband, mentor,** and sometimes all of them at once.

During my time as a student assistant at Penn State, I was blessed with the opportunity to become the head football coach at Simon Gratz, the same high school I once dropped out of. That year, I found something deeper than football; I discovered purpose in people. I realized how much I loved developing others, sharing my faith, and showing kids from neighborhoods like mine that they could succeed through discipline, education, and belief. We finished the season 8-4, but the real victory was in how many lives were changed by seeing someone who looked like them come back as a college graduate and a man of God.

After just one season back in North Philadelphia as a high school head coach, I was offered my first full-time collegiate head strength and assistant coaching position at Cheyney University. Resources were limited, and challenges were everywhere, much like Simon Gratz. But in that struggle, I grew as a **leader, a coach, and a father**. After spending two years at the University of Cheyney, my family and I relocated to **Melbourne Beach, Florida**, where I served as **assistant head coach, offensive coordinator, strength and conditioning coach, and gym teacher** at Melbourne High School.

Florida brought new lessons. I gained insight into **game planning, school structure, dealing with parents**, and managing a program from a broader lens. We went to the **playoffs two years in a row**, and my passion for **strength and conditioning** deepened. I realized I could **develop young men even more effectively off the field than on it.**

And in the middle of it all, life happened.

By the time I left Melbourne, **my wife had earned her cosmetology license**, achieving her dream. And we had four children, **three girls and one son, Gus "EJ" Felder Jr.**, who was **born at halftime** of a rivalry homecoming game against **Eau Gallie High School**. Earlier that day, my wife, Kelly, had come to the game to support me, as she always did. But partway through the first quarter, she began experiencing strong contractions and had to leave early to have our son.

What made the situation even more unique was that the doctor delivering our baby, Dr. Wolk, was also the father of our starting middle linebacker. As I coached the first half, my father-in-law Jim, with the help of Dr. Wolk, kept me updated from the sideline on Kelly's condition. The timing couldn't have been tighter. As soon as the halftime whistle blew, Dr. Wolk and I rushed down the street to Melbourne Hospital, just minutes from the field. By the time I arrived, labor was fully underway. That night, we won the game 6–0 with the only touchdown coming on a gritty run. But even more unforgettable was what happened off the field: I became a father again. That game and that day will always hold a special place in my heart.

Soon, I left Melbourne because my **temporary teacher certification expired**, and I didn't have enough time to meet the state's permanent licensure requirements. But the lessons I learned there stayed with me. It all prepared me for what came next: returning to **Penn State University**—this time not as a student or player, but as a graduate **strength and conditioning coach under John Thomas**.

That whole stretch from Philly to Florida was full of transition, pressure, and nonstop motion. But what grounded me through all of it…was **stillness**. Not physical stillness, but mental and spiritual stillness, through family, support, and building **LEGO**. The kind you get when you slow down, breathe, and hear God speak.

Spiritual Devotion

"Be still, and know that I am God."
Psalm 46:10

When your plate is full, kids to raise, athletes to coach, games to win, and bills to pay, **stillness can feel like a luxury.** But the truth is, it's a necessity.

God doesn't shout over the noise; He speaks through the quiet.

Every time I paused to pray, to reflect, to sit with His Word, He reminded me: *You are not what you do. You are who I've called you to be.*

Stillness didn't take the challenges away. It gave me the **perspective and strength to walk through them with purpose.**

The Leadership Lesson

In leadership, especially in athletics, **motion is constant.** But growth doesn't just come from speed, it comes from **intentional stillness.**

Stillness gives you the emotional space to make better decisions. It gives you clarity in chaos. And most importantly, it reminds you that **your strength isn't just physical, it's spiritual.**

Whether you're in a weight room, a classroom, a home, or a boardroom, **stillness can be your greatest advantage.**

The Challenge to the Reader

Where do you need to slow down?

Are you chasing approval instead of purpose?

Are you running on empty, trying to prove something?

When's the last time you stopped just to breathe and listen?

This week, carve out 10 minutes a day to sit in stillness. Just you and God. No phone. No pressure. No agenda.

Now pray:

> *"Lord, in the rush of life, teach me to be still. Help me pause, listen, and trust that Your voice is louder than my circumstances. Quiet my heart so I can lead with wisdom, not just hustle. Remind me that stillness isn't weakness, it's where true strength begins. Amen."*

Because the **loudest breakthroughs often begin in the quietest moments.**

And the **strongest leaders** aren't always the loudest in the room; they're the ones who know how to be still and still stand strong.

†

†

†

†

5

KNOW THYSELF

Stoic Quote:

"He who conquers himself is the mightiest warrior."
CONFUCIUS

TITLES COME AND GO. Jerseys are taken off. Whistles are handed over. But one question always remains: **Who are you when the lights go off?**

I've worn a lot of labels: **athlete, coach, husband, father, mentor.** Each one has shaped me. But the seasons where I grew the most were the ones that stripped those labels away and forced me to look in the mirror, not at my achievements, but at my character.

After coaching at Simon Gratz and taking my first college coaching and strength job at Cheyney University, I believed I was moving up. However, I soon learned that growth doesn't always feel like success. I was commuting over an hour and a half each morning from Philadelphia to Cheyney, leaving my wife and young children behind every day. For two years, I sacrificed time, presence, and peace in an effort to provide for my family. And even though it strengthened us in the long run, it was emotionally and spiritually draining.

During that time, I **missed birthdays, funerals, and quiet moments** that I'll never get back. I **lost close friends and family**, not because of a falling out but because **I wasn't present**, and life moved on without me. **Death in silence.** I carried that grief quietly. But God used that pain to teach me about **fellowship, parenthood, and brotherhood.** It forced me to slow down and reconsider what really mattered.

Then came **Melbourne High School** in Florida. I poured everything into that program, developing young men, organizing game plans, and guiding families. But I also faced another test: my **teaching certification expired**, and I couldn't complete the necessary requirements in time. We suddenly found ourselves in a **deep financial hole.**

My wife and I packed up our growing family, now with four children, and moved back to **State College, Pennsylvania**. With nowhere else to go, we moved into my mother's **three-bedroom townhome**, which was already occupied. There were seven people under one roof.

We lost things that mattered at the time:

My truck was repossessed.

Our privacy disappeared.

My pride took a hit.

But we kept our **faith.** And that faith was enough.

I volunteered in the **Penn State weight room** under John Thomas for a few months, unpaid, just showing up, putting in the work. Eventually, I was offered a **graduate assistant role** and later earned my **first master's degree in Health Education**. I fell in love with **strength and conditioning**, but even more than that, I found myself as a **mentor, leader, older**

brother, father figure, and friend to young men and women chasing their own breakthroughs.

That year, **2009,** taught me how to stop striving for external validation and start living from internal conviction. It taught me **perseverance, patience, peace**, and most importantly, how to lead from identity, not insecurity.

After three seasons at Penn State, I was offered a new opportunity: **Director of Strength and Conditioning and Offensive Line Coach at Clark Atlanta University**. We packed up again and drove from State College to **Atlanta, Georgia**, stepping into another chapter with deeper faith and a stronger foundation. While in Atlanta, our faith grew stronger, and I could see clearly who I was and how God was leading my life.

Spiritual Devotion

"I have been crucified with Christ and I no longer live, but Christ lives in me."
GALATIANS 2:20

God doesn't waste anything, not loss, not hardship, not pain. Every moment, from the long drives and the repo'd truck to the crowded apartment and the silence of grief, was part of His refining process. While the world tells us to find ourselves in success, the kingdom of God invites us to lose ourselves in Christ. And it's in that surrender, in that loss, that **we truly discover who we are.**

The Leadership Lesson

You can't lead others if you don't know yourself.

Self-awareness isn't just about personality tests or motivational speeches; it's about **knowing your values when everything is stripped away.** It's about remembering who you are when no one else sees your work.

The best leaders don't lead from platforms; they lead from the foundation of **identity, tested and true.**

The Challenge to the Reader

Who are you really?

What painful experience might God be using to reveal your character?

Where have you confused performance with purpose?

What part of your identity needs to be surrendered?

This week, take time to sit with the hard question:

If everything were taken from me, what would still be true about who I am?

Now pray:

"Lord, when life strips away the titles and the applause, help me stand firm in who You say I am. Remind me that my identity isn't in what I do, but in who I am becoming. Thank you for using the pain, the quiet, and the unseen work to shape my character. Let me lead with humility, grounded in purpose, not pride. Amen."

Because you're not your job. You're not your wins or losses. You are who God says you are, even when no one else sees it. And **that is enough.**

†

†

†

†

6

BROTHERHOOD, NOT JUST TEAMMATES

Stoic Quote:
"We are all limbs of one body."
Seneca

When people think about college football, they picture roaring crowds and weight-room bravado. What they rarely see is the quiet **brotherhood** that keeps young men standing when everything else feels shaky.

For me, that brotherhood started **before I ever earned my scholarship**. The summer bridge program that got me into Penn State paired me with a roommate named **Aaron Rice**. Aaron *wasn't* a football player; he was simply a good-hearted guy from tiny **Mount Union, PA,** who could relate to the kid from North Philly trying to find his footing.

While I battled non-qualifier status and the pressure to prove myself, Aaron became a refuge. We pulled all-nighters over math flashcards, had late-night talks about faith and family, and on weekends drove out to Mount Union to eat with his folks and breathe small-town air. He reminded me that I was more than an eligibility label or depth-chart slot; I was a man worth believing in.

Then came the teammates who turned into **lifelong brothers**: **Anthony "Spice" Adams** and **Bryant "BJ" Johnson**. From the day we arrived in 1998, we sharpened each other on the field, in class, and in the Word. They all went on to long NFL careers (eight to ten years apiece), yet our bond never became a highlight-reel footnote.

Spice: As life went on and we grew older and developed a better bond with each other, he would FaceTime to check out a new video idea he had, uplift me with his unusually God-given gift of making people laugh, to make sure I was working out, and to pray with me before big decisions.

BJ: is the reason I later felt bold enough to uproot my family and reboot our lives in Georgia; we'd already spent years pouring courage into each other. BJ was the little big brother I needed, always giving the best advice, and included me in his circle of NFL friends who all sought unbiased guidance from someone not looking to gain anything from them.

To my kids, they're **Uncle Spice and Uncle BJ**. They celebrated my early marriage and fatherhood when most college students were still choosing majors. Later, when their NFL journeys cooled and my coaching path heated up from high school sidelines to Power 5 locker rooms, they called to ask *my* advice on marriage, parenting, and walking with Christ. Brotherhood is a two-way street.

These men and many more whose names would fill pages prove a simple truth: championships fade, but **covenant friendships** echo for decades.

Spiritual Devotion

"As iron sharpens iron, so one person sharpens another."
Proverbs 27:17

Scripture never describes discipleship as a solo sport. God forges character in **community** through honest conversations, shared burdens, and the kind of loyalty that shows up unannounced. My brothers were God's carpenters, shaving off pride, sanding down insecurity, and strengthening my faith grain by grain.

The Leadership Lesson

Great leaders don't rise alone; they **rise with and for others**. Brotherhood:

Anchors identity friends who say, "Remember who you are."

Challenges complacency, teammates who refuse to let you coast.

Multiplies impact because one faithful man becomes four, then forty.

If you want a winning culture, build genuine relationships first; strategy follows the strength of those connections.

The Challenge to the Reader

Name your Aaron. Who quietly carries your backpack when life gets heavy? Thank them this week.

Reach out to a Spice or BJ. Encourage a brother (or sister) who once encouraged you.

Be that person for someone younger, invite them into your circle, your home, your prayers.

Now pray:

> *"Father, Thank You for the brothers who lift us, sharpen us, and walk beside us. Teach me to be that kind of friend, steady, loyal, and true. Help me value relationships over recognition, and remember that a real legacy is found in how we build each other up. Amen."*

Because trophies tarnish, records fall, and titles change, but **brotherhood endures, and it makes us all stronger limbs of the same body.**

†

†

†

7

STAND TALL IN THE FIRE

Stoic Quote:

"Fire is the test of gold; adversity, of strong men."
Seneca

There are seasons in life that feel like they're designed to break you. You wake up in a storm, and it's not going away. No quick fix. No easy out. Just fire.

I've had my share of wins, state titles, college football milestones, raising a family, and walking in purpose. But the seasons that truly revealed who I was weren't the ones where I stood on podiums. They were the ones who scorched everything but my faith.

There were years when I was coaching by day and grieving by night, **losing close friends and family members quietly**, with no time to mourn, because life kept moving and people still needed me to lead.

There were days when I drove **hours each way to Cheyney University**, physically exhausted, emotionally depleted, but still showing up for the athletes who depended on me, all while **missing irreplaceable moments with my wife and kids**.

There was the stretch in **Melbourne**, where, after not securing my full teaching license in time, we had to **leave everything**

behind, move into my mom's crowded townhome, and start from scratch. **My truck was repossessed**, my bank account was empty, and the pressure to provide was crushing.

There was the pain of being **overlooked for promotions**, passed up for jobs, or let go without warning after pouring heart and soul into players and programs.

Each time, I had two choices:

Let the fire consume me.

Let the fire refine me.

I chose the second one sometimes barely, but consistently. I remained rooted in God's promises, even when my emotions didn't align with my faith. And every fire made me **stronger, wiser, and more dependent on the One who walks through the flames with me.**

Spiritual Devotion

> *"When you walk through the fire, you will not be burned; the flames will not set you ablaze."*
> Isaiah 43:2

God never promised we wouldn't face fire. He promised we wouldn't face it **alone**.

He doesn't use comfort to develop leaders. He uses **pressure**, **testing**, and **loss** to strip away ego, expose character, and build endurance.

When I was at my lowest, broke, grieving, and doubting, God wasn't absent. He was working. And every fire He allowed was a furnace to **burn away what wasn't necessary**, so I could emerge with clarity, faith, and strength that no job, title, or applause could give me.

The Leadership Lesson

Fire reveals. Always. It shows what's fake and what's forged.

True leaders aren't shaped on stage, they're shaped in the **quiet fires of faith and failure**. The ones who last are the ones who learned to keep showing up **when no one's cheering and everything hurts**.

If you want to lead at a high level, you've got to be willing to go through seasons where **God is the only one clapping.**

The Challenge to the Reader

Are you in a fire season right now?

Are you tempted to quit because it's hard?

Are you trying to escape something God might be using to develop you?

Are you waiting for the pain to end instead of looking for the lesson within it?

Write this down somewhere visible:

"This fire is forming me, not finishing me."

Now pray:

> *"Lord, when life gets hot and the pressure rises, help me to remember that You are with me in the flames. Teach me to stand tall not because I'm strong, but because You are. Use every hardship to refine me, not break me. Make me better, not bitter. And let my scars become strength for someone else's storm. Amen."*

And remember: fire doesn't mean failure, it implies **refining**. Keep standing. Keep believing. **Stand tall in the fire.**

†

†

8

THE LOCKER ROOM PULPIT

Stoic Quote:

"Waste no more time arguing what a good man should be. Be one."
Marcus Aurelius

I'VE NEVER NEEDED A MICROPHONE or a church pulpit to share the Word. **The locker room has always been my sanctuary.**

I learned early that if you show up with consistency, love, and truth, people will listen, even when you never open a Bible. Throughout my years as a coach, strength leader, and mentor, I've seen the locker room transform into a sacred space, a place where young men wrestle with purpose, identity, anger, grief, faith, and dreams.

They don't always come in asking for guidance.

Sometimes they need someone to look them in the eye and say, *"You matter"*.

Sometimes, it's catching a player after practice who's walking with his head down and saying, *"You're more than your last mistake."*

Sometimes, it's sitting in a coach's office with a player who's questioning his life and reminding him, *"You're not alone."*

And sometimes it's just **living in a way that makes people curious about your peace.**

That's what I've worked to do for over two decades. Whether it was at **Clark Atlanta, UGA, Miami, or Nebraska**, I never led with a sermon. From my morning staff devotions at Clark Atlanta and Miami, where I led with Jermey Roberts, I met Jeremy while coaching at Clark Atlanta. He started out as one of my athletes, and I recall that we spent a considerable amount of time recruiting him, as he had come to us from the University of South Alabama.

Jeremy Roberts was a young man working to establish himself as a solid graduate football player. God connected us that season, knowing we needed each other at that time. His father was a bishop from Mobile, Alabama, and he was grounded and rooted in God's word. Jeremy went from being a student-athlete to my assistant at Clark Atlanta, Miami, and Bethlehem Christian Academy. Moreover, he was the spiritual leader God sent to me when I needed God's teachings the most. With him, I was able to learn and demonstrate presence. Because presence builds trust, and **trust opens hearts.**

Faith isn't something I turn off when I put on a team T-shirt; it's who I am. And over time, people noticed. They started coming to me not just for reps or game plans, but for advice on **relationships, fatherhood, addiction, prayer, and pain.**

That's when I knew this was **my pulpit.**

Spiritual Devotion

"In the same way, let your light shine before others, that they may see your good deeds and glorify your Father in heaven."
Matthew 5:16

Some people wait for the right setting to minister. But leadership *is* ministry, especially when you serve with humility and conviction.

God doesn't always need your words; sometimes He just needs your walk.

Every weight room becomes holy ground when you approach it with purpose. Every meeting room can become a counseling center when you're willing to listen. **Every locker room can be a pulpit** if your life preaches louder than your lips.

The Leadership Lesson

You don't need a title to lead.

You don't need a pulpit to preach.

You don't need perfection to influence.

You need **authenticity**. You need **presence**. You need **consistency**.

Players don't remember every drill or every win. But they'll never forget the leader who showed up for them as a **man of character**, not just a coach of schemes.

The Challenge to the Reader

Where is your pulpit?

Is it your classroom?
Your job?
Your home?
Your team?

Don't wait for a spotlight to start making a difference. Let your integrity be your sermon. Let your consistency be your testimony.

This week, commit to one quiet act of leadership that preaches louder than any words:

> A note of encouragement
> A word of truth
> A moment of listening
> A prayer behind the scenes

Now pray:

> *"Lord, help me lead not just with words, but with the way I live. Let my presence carry peace, my actions reflect truth, and my consistency build trust. Whether I'm in a locker room, classroom, or kitchen, let my life speak louder than my voice. Make me a living message of grace, strength, and love. Amen."*

Because someone is watching your life and asking, *"Is this real?"*

Let your answer be **how you lead every day**.

†

†

9

FATHERHOOD IS LEGACY

Stoic Quote:

"Don't stumble over something behind you."
SENECA

SCOREBOARDS FADE AND TROPHIES TARNISH, but the stories our children tell about us echo for generations. My legacy isn't the rings I've chased or the rosters I've led; it's the lives that call me *Dad*, husband, unc, friend, brother, BigDawg, and coach long after the stadium lights shut off.

Destiny, who's now 28 years old, is my firstborn and my first real teacher. As a college student juggling marriage, parenthood, classes, and football, I thought I knew "grind" until Destiny arrived. **She taught me patient love, late-night bottle drills, and the art of laughing at chaos. Bright, driven, and analytical, she processes the world the way I do and still challenges me to grow.**

Jazmin, my second baby, who is now 23 years old, has blessed me with two grandsons, Travell (4) and Takodah (1). I see my own mother's fearless honesty in her everyday life. She speaks truth like a lightning bolt, yet carries a soft heart that would give anyone the clothes off her back. **She is a loving daughter and friend who wears her love on her sleeves. Jaz reminds me that compassion and courage are twins.**

Alexa, my sweet 21-year-old, is my **perpetual adventure buddy. She approaches life with a light spirit, reminding her over-serious dad to breathe.** She asks questions, tags along everywhere, and sees the wonder that I sometimes miss.

Gus "EJ" Eric James, my 16-year-old and only son, was a long-awaited blessing after I prayed for a son following three daughters and a few failed pregnancies. Then God blessed us with EJ. **He's an honor-roll student, a protective brother, a budding teammate and friend, and a reflection of my mannerisms.** He's figuring out where he fits in both the game and in life. Watching him test his gifts with patience and passion might be my favorite coaching assignment yet.

Faith Jade, my last blessing, is now 14 years old. She is one of our miracle babies. After doctors warned us against having more pregnancies, God had other plans. **Faith is a talented artist and problem-solver who listens deeply and dreams loudly.** She and EJ remind me that every "no" mankind speaks is still subject to God's "yes."

The good Lord has blessed us with five beautiful children, born of eleven pregnancies, teaching my wife, Kelly, and me to trust God's timing and remain grateful for every heartbeat entrusted to us. Raising a biracial family in America hasn't always been easy. Many voices have tried to pull us apart, but grace has kept us welded together. And football kept my heart young. It also expanded our household:

Justin Evans, a New Jersey native we met at Nebraska, became an adopted son in spirit.

Haley Rogers entered our lives at eight years old and is now a thriving 21-year-old. We are proud to call her our daughter.

Scores of players from Simon Gratz, Cheyney, Melbourne, Clark Atlanta, UGA, Miami, Nebraska, Penn State, State College High, and many NFL team members still reach out for wisdom, workouts, or wedding advice.

Biological or not, God keeps enlarging our table, and we wouldn't have it any other way.

Spiritual Devotion

"Start children off on the way they should go, and even when they are old, they will not turn from it."
Proverbs 22:6

Fatherhood is discipleship in denim and cleats. The goal isn't to manufacture mini-me's; it's to launch image-bearers into their God-written callings. Every bedtime prayer, every sideline hug, every hard conversation is a seed in soil I may never fully see, but legacy is measured in forests, not saplings.

The Leadership Lesson

True influence is generational. Championships gather dust, but a son who prays with his team or a daughter who gives away her shoes, that's leadership reproducing itself. A leader's résumé should read like a family tree: branches spreading wider than his reach.

The Challenge to the Reader

Name your heirs. Biological, mentee, student, niece, who will carry your values forward?

Invest today. Send the text, share the wisdom, show up at the recital.

Choose legacy over résumé. Ask: *Will this decision matter to the people who call me family?*

Now pray:

> *"Heavenly Father, thank you for the gift of the legacy of shaping lives not just through our words, but through how we love, lead, and show up. Teach me to see every moment with my children, my players, and those I mentor as sacred. Help me plant seeds of faith, strength, and compassion, even when the harvest is far off. Let my life echo in the generations that follow. Amen."*

Because someday, your greatest stat line won't be wins and losses, it will be the stories your children (and their children) tell about how you loved, led, and lived.

†

†

†

10

ONE TEAM, ONE VISION

Stoic Quote:

"No man is an island."
INSPIRED BY THE STOIC PRINCIPLE OF COMMUNAL DUTY

I'VE COACHED PLAYERS FROM EVERY WALK OF LIFE, inner-city athletes and small-town kids, five-star recruits and overlooked walk-ons, future pros and first-time starters. Talent alone doesn't build a great team. **Unity does.**

One of the greatest lessons I've learned in leadership is this: **no matter how skilled individuals are, if they don't share the same vision, the team will collapse.**

From my early years coaching at **Simon Gratz** to college jobs at **Cheyney, Clark Atlanta, UGA, Miami, Nebraska**, and even at the **NFL level with the Carolina Panthers,** the teams that thrived weren't just talented. They were **connected**. They bought into a culture, a mission, and most importantly, into each other.

I've seen what happens when people pursue personal stats instead of collective success. I've also witnessed the beauty of what occurs when a group of men chooses "we" over "me," when the O-line celebrates a running back's touchdown as if it were their own, when coaches hold each other accountable off the field. When support staff are treated with the same respect as coordinators, that's where culture is built. I have been privileged to serve alongside some of the game's greatest culture builders, including Coach Mark Richt and Coach Matt Rhule.

This applies far beyond the field. In my **marriage**, Kelly and I have endured two decades of ups, downs, relocations, lost pregnancies, and financial pressure. But our strength was never about comfort; it was about **shared vision**. We made a choice early on: no matter what comes, we're not opponents. We're **teammates**.

It's the same with my kids. Each one is unique with different personalities, gifts, and challenges, but they all know the same truth: in this house, **we pull together, not apart.**

Vision keeps teams from drifting. Alignment keeps it from crumbling. And when a leader is clear and consistent about purpose, everyone else finds their role more confidently.

Spiritual Devotion

"Two are better than one, because they have a good return for their labor... Though one may be overpowered, two can defend themselves. A cord of three strands is not quickly broken."
ECCLESIASTES 4:9,12

God doesn't call us to walk alone. He designed us for **teamwork** with Him, with each other, and with a purpose bigger than personal ambition.

Where there is **no vision**, people scatter; however, where there is a shared purpose in marriage, in mentorship, or in ministry, **His power multiplies.**

The Leadership Lesson

If you want a high-performing team, **define the vision clearly** and **build the culture daily**. Vision leaks, so it must be refilled regularly through conversations, corrections, celebrations, and consistency.

Great leaders:

    Cast vision people can see themselves in

    Create space for people to bring their full selves

    Lead with **clarity, humility, and conviction**

Unity isn't automatic. It's cultivated. And it requires a **leader who doesn't just talk to the team but lives it.**

The Challenge to the Reader

Who are you trying to lead right now, and are you all aiming at the same goal?

Ask yourself:

Does my team (home, work, staff) know the vision?

Am I leading with clarity or just busyness?

What's one thing I can do this week to unite my people around a shared mission?

Now pray:

> *"Lord, Thank You for the teams you've placed in my life at home, at work, and on the field. Help me lead with clarity, love, and shared purpose. Teach me to value every role, celebrate every contribution, and build a culture rooted in unity. May we move as one: one team, one heartbeat, one vision. Amen."*

Because **vision without unity** is just noise. But when people unite under a clear, purpose-driven banner?

That's when something special happens. Trust in **One team. One heartbeat. One vision.**

†

†

†

11

THE POWER OF PRESENCE

Stoic Quote:

"Be here now."
INSPIRED BY THE STOIC PRINCIPLE OF MINDFULNESS

ONE OF THE GREATEST GIFTS GOD HAS EVER GIVEN ME isn't money, status, or accolades; it's the ability to **be present**.

In this world of constant motion, phones buzzing, schedules packed, and noise everywhere, presence is rare. But presence is where miracles happen. A close friend and spiritual brother of mine, **Pastor Thomas Settles of Calvary Church in Athens, Georgia**, once told me something that shook me deeply:

"You may be the only Bible some people ever read."

That statement changed me. It reminded me that how I live, how I speak, how I serve, and how I show up might be the only glimpse of God that someone ever sees. Therefore, I've tried, though not perfectly, but intentionally to live in a way that honors that responsibility.

God didn't make me perfect. I've had struggles, wounds, and disappointments. But he's used every single one of them not to punish me, but to **position me** to be a blessing to others. My presence in homes, locker rooms, sideline huddles, and quiet conversations isn't about me. It's about what **God wants to do through me** in that moment.

I've seen this power in my **family**, especially with my children and wife. Being present isn't just attending games or dinners. It's about showing up emotionally, listening, praying, hugging, forgiving, and growing.

I've seen it in my brothers Kendrick, Kevin, and Jamel. Each of us carries our own weight, our own memories, and our own path. However, by being more present in each other's lives, we can give one another strength. We lift each other up and live in ways that make our parents in heaven proud. I've witnessed this in the most unexpected places: in hallways, weight rooms, and quiet sideline moments where God orchestrated encounters I didn't even know were coming. Conversations about suicide, fatherhood, faith, and forgiveness…moments when someone's entire life shifted simply because I was in the right place at the right time and was paying attention. That's the power of presence.

Spiritual Devotion

"Therefore, as God's chosen people... clothe yourselves with compassion, kindness, humility, gentleness and patience."
Colossians 3:12

Jesus never hurried past people. He stopped. He saw. He listened. His presence healed, comforted, and gave purpose.

When you are fully present in spirit, not just in body, **you become an extension of God's love.**

Every encounter becomes an opportunity for grace. Every moment becomes holy ground.

The Leadership Lesson

Being present doesn't require a title, a stage, or a plan. It requires **attention**, **compassion**, and **availability**.

The best leaders:

Listen when no one else does

Notice what others overlook

Create space for breakthrough moments

Presence is a ministry all by itself.

The Challenge to the Reader

Where are you rushing through life and missing opportunities to be present?

Are you in the room but not really *in* the moment?

Who needs your full attention, not your advice, just your presence?

What would it look like to show up for others the way God shows up for you?

Now pray:

"Father, Thank You for the reminder that presence is powerful. Help me to slow down, listen well, and show up for those around me, not just in body but in spirit. Let my life reflect Your love in quiet moments, in hallway talks, in family time, and in times of pain. May I be the Bible someone else needs to read today. Amen."

This week, slow down. Look up. **Be the Bible someone else needs to read.**

Because presence, not perfection, is often what people remember most.

†

†

†

12

BEYOND THE FINAL WHISTLE

Stoic Quote:

"Life is long if you know how to use it."
SENECA

THERE'S A MOMENT EVERY COMPETITOR eventually faces the end of the game. The final whistle blows, the stadium clears out, and the uniform comes off. And the question becomes: **what now?** For me, the answer didn't come immediately. It came quietly, during a late-night discussion while pursuing my doctoral degree at the University of Nebraska. A professor posed a question that gripped my spirit:

"What will your influence look like 100 years from now?"

That question didn't ask about trophies. It didn't care about sideline wins or job titles. It asked about the **legacy** of the echo of your life long after you're gone. And it stirred something in me that had been growing for years.

I love the game of football. It changed my life. But what I've grown to love even more is the **development of people**. From being a strength coach to a player development leader, from coaching on Friday nights to walking players through fatherhood and finances, I realized the real scoreboard was always **off the field**.

So I sat down and started writing. I didn't write a to-do list. I wrote a **legacy plan**.

I envisioned launching a leadership institute that would serve under-resourced high school coaches—the ones who have the heart but lack the help.

I dreamed of publishing research on holistic player development, bridging athletics and academics for long-term success.

I committed to establishing scholarships for **first-generation student-athletes** because I know what it means to be the first in your family to believe you belong.

And I didn't stop there. I began mapping out the steps, naming the partners, aligning the timelines, writing the vision down, and making it plain.

But more than just a plan, I started living like legacy mattered today.

That means loving my wife with intention, so our kids see what commitment really looks like. It means mentoring my brothers, Kendrick, Kevin, and Jamel, and encouraging each of them to lead their families with faith and strength. It means pouring into young men like Justin Evans and Jeremy Roberts, our extended family, because every seed you plant can bloom in a life you never expected.

Beyond the final whistle is not about retiring from the game; it's about realizing that your real work is just beginning.

Spiritual Devotion

"I have fought the good fight, I have finished the race, I have kept the faith."
2 Timothy 4:7

When Paul wrote those words, he wasn't talking about a game, a career, or a title. He was talking about **purpose fulfilled.**

Finishing doesn't mean you stop running. It means you run your portion with everything you've got, and then you pass the baton.

The work God calls you to doesn't end with applause; it ends with **impact.**

And the beauty of His plan is this: the race doesn't stop when you do. It continues through the people you've loved, led, and lifted.

The Leadership Lesson

Legacy is not an accident. It's a decision backed by action, sacrifice, and faith.

Your title will fade. Your impact won't. Don't wait for a platform to lead where you stand.

Finish lines are not dead ends. They're **launchpads** for the next generation.

Your story isn't meant to be bookmarked at retirement; it's meant to be **passed on.**

The Challenge to the Reader

Take 20 minutes and write your **Legacy Letter**. Include:

Who will carry your values?

What resources or wisdom will you leave them?

How are you preparing them at the moment?

Now pray:

> *"Lord, help me live with the end in mind and eternity in my heart. Teach me to value impact over applause, and purpose over position. Let my days be filled with meaningful work that outlives me. Give me vision for legacy, clarity in planning, and the courage to lead now, not later. May those I've mentored rise stronger, go farther, and carry Your truth because I chose to invest in more than wins, I chose to invest in people. Amen."*

Don't wait for the perfect season to begin. Start building the legacy God assigned to you now.

Because after the final whistle, after the stadium lights go out...the **inside game** still lives on in those you've poured into, loved well, and led with purpose.

†

†

†

13

BUILD BUILDERS

Stoic Quote:

"What we do now echoes in eternity."
MARCUS AURELIUS

BY THE TIME I STEPPED INTO THE ROLE of Executive Director of Player Development at the University of Nebraska, I had worn just about every hat in football: player, coach, strength trainer, and mentor. But this was different. This time, I wasn't just developing athletes. I was building people.

And not just players, **staff, interns, young coaches, even myself.**

There were no more whistles or squat racks. Instead, I had a whiteboard, a calendar, and a mandate to shape men from the inside out. That's when **"The Readiness Program"** was born, a 12-month curriculum focused on developing the complete student-athlete: mentally, emotionally, spiritually, and socially.

Every week, we held sessions on emotional intelligence, financial literacy, servant leadership, and spiritual discipline. We challenged our young men to be vulnerable, honest, and hungry for growth, not just as athletes, but as **husbands, fathers, leaders, and men of faith.** To enhance the impact, my head coach and friend supported me wholeheartedly.

We saw results fast. GPAs climbed. Locker room drama dropped. Practice tempo improved not because we changed the drills, but because we **changed the culture.** These young men felt seen, heard, and supported. They knew their value wasn't just tied to a depth chart.

And the day one of my student assistants stood up to lead the weekly devotion without being asked, that was the moment I knew something deeper had taken root. **That's leadership. That's legacy.** It's not about how loud your voice is, it's about how long your impact echoes after you've left the room.

Spiritual Devotion

"And the things you have heard me say ... entrust to reliable people who will also be qualified to teach others."
2 Timothy 2:2

Leadership was never meant to stop with you.

Jesus didn't just perform miracles; He multiplied them by pouring into the disciples and **equipping them to go and do likewise.**

That's the model. The goal isn't to create followers. The goal is to **create more leaders.**

And that takes time. It takes trust. It takes humility.

If you're always the hero of your own story, you're not building builders. You're just building dependency.

The Leadership Lesson

True success in leadership is measured by the ability to create a successful succession. If everything rises and falls on you, then you haven't truly led; you've hoarded. Great culture doesn't happen by accident; it must be structured. Intentional systems will always outlast motivational slogans. Write the process, calendar it, and commit to it. And above all, equip, empower, and then release. Great leaders don't grip the mic; they pass it on. Because legacy leadership isn't about leaving something behind; it's about leaving someone ready.

The Challenge to the Reader

Look around you. Who in your circle needs what you've learned the hard way?

Choose **one person** to train up this month in a key responsibility you currently hold.

Teach them. Trust them. Let them lead it once without your shadow looming.

Then step back. **Observe. Encourage. Empower.**

Now pray:

"Father God, thank You for the opportunity to lead beyond the surface, to develop hearts, not just habits. Teach me to invest in others with intentionality, to see beyond performance and into purpose. Help me raise up leaders who carry vision, character, and conviction long after I'm gone. Let my words, my work, and my witness leave an echo that multiplies. Give me wisdom to structure the process, grace to step back, and courage to trust those I'm building. Lord, make me a builder of builders. Amen."

Because if the work dies when you step away, you haven't built something eternal; you've built something temporary.

Real impact isn't measured in how many people follow you. It's measured in how many people you can lead when you're gone.

†

†

†

14

THE HEALTH EQUATION: LEADING FROM THE INSIDE OUT

Stoic Quote:

"No man has the right to be an amateur in the matter of physical training."
SOCRATES

FOR MOST OF MY LIFE, training focused on performance on the field, in the weight room, and under the lights. As a player, strength coach, and leader, I embraced the "bigger, faster, stronger" mentality. That mindset carried me through years of competition and coaching. However, over time, I began to realize that true strength wasn't just about how much you could lift; it was about how well you could live.

It struck me during a conversation with my brother, Bryant Johnson, after visiting Atlanta in 2012. I was tired—not just physically, but also mentally and spiritually. And I realized something: I had devoted so much time to helping others build strong bodies, sharpen their minds, and establish disciplined routines...but I hadn't been intentionally training myself for life beyond the whistle. With the push and support of my brother BJ, I made a decision not because something was wrong, but because something needed to be better.

I began training for a lifestyle of leadership and longevity. That meant prioritizing sleep, even during the grind of the season, because a **rested mind makes clearer, more informed decisions**. It meant eating to fuel my calling, not following a strict diet, but making more purposeful choices: more whole foods, less sugar and junk, and a greater sense of balance. I committed to moving daily, not just to stay strong, but to stay free, whether through walks, lifting, stretching, or breathing, whatever would help keep my body and mind in alignment. I also started making time for my family, not just being physically present, but emotionally present as well, laughing, listening, and soaking in the small moments that matter most. And here's where it got special: my wife, Kelly, was right there with me.

We didn't just encourage each other, we **trained together**. Our journey into powerlifting became more than just a hobby. It was a shared mission. Mornings at the gym before the world woke up. Spotting each other on squats, cheering for each other on deadlifts. Competing side-by-side in local meets. We weren't just getting stronger physically; we were strengthening our marriage, our friendship, our trust.

There's something powerful about pushing past your limits **together,** especially when the person beside you has been with you through every season of life. From two teenagers at Job Corps trying to figure it out, to a married couple raising five children, to a powerlifting duo still chasing personal bests, we were proving that strength is **a shared pursuit.**

What changed wasn't just our routine; it was our **rhythm.** We were choosing to honor our health as an act of love, stewardship, and legacy.

The benefits weren't just physical. I was more patient, more energized, and more focused. Kelly was more confident, more joyful, more empowered. And it impacted everyone around us, from our athletes and colleagues to our kids and community. We started preaching something new in the weight room:

"Train for life. Train to lead. Train to finish strong."

Spiritual Devotion

"Do you not know that your bodies are temples of the Holy Spirit?"
1 Corinthians 6:19

We serve a God who moves through vessels. Sometimes, the condition of our vessel affects how far and how fast we can go. Your body is not just flesh and bone; it's a vehicle of purpose. Taking care of it is not vanity; it's stewardship. Whether you're leading in sports, in church, in the classroom, or at home, how you treat your body influences how you show up for your assignment. This is not about perfection; it's about intention.

The Leadership Lesson

Lead yourself first. You can't expect discipline from your team if you're not living it.

Sustainable habits matter. You don't need a diet, you need a rhythm. You don't need a perfect plan, you need a consistent one.

Your presence is your greatest gift. Being healthy, whole, and available will impact more lives than any playbook ever could.

The Challenge to the Reader

What part of your personal health have you been putting on the back burner?

Pick one area: **sleep, movement, nutrition, rest, or relationships,** and set a 30-day goal. It doesn't need to be drastic. Just deliberate.

Maybe it's getting 7 hours of sleep. Maybe it's walking every morning. Maybe it's putting the phone away at dinner. God will help you decide.

Now pray:

"Heavenly Father, thank You for the gift of this body, this vessel You've entrusted to carry out Your purpose. Help me steward it well. Teach me to prioritize rest without guilt, to eat with intention, to move with joy, and to live with balance. Strengthen not just my muscles, but my mind and spirit. Bless the rhythm of my life and marriage, and may our health be a reflection of Your goodness and grace. Let my discipline be a testimony to others that leadership begins with self-care. In Jesus' name, Amen."

Then ask yourself this:

"If I treated my health like it was a part of my leadership legacy…what would I do differently?"

Because the stronger you are **inside**, the more impact you'll have on everyone watching from the outside.

†

†

†

†

15

FINISH WITH FIRE

Stoic Quote:

*"Death smiles at us all.
All a man can do is smile back."*
Marcus Aurelius

In 1996, two 16-year-olds, Kelly and I, met with more hope than history. By **2000**, we stood before God, the Pastor, and the congregation and promised, *"Til death do us part."* Now it's **2025, 25 years of marriage**, five children, two grandchildren, eleven pregnancies, dozens of zip codes, and a lifetime of highs and lows later, and we're still holding hands and finishing what we started.

"**Finish**" has been the drumbeat of my life. I started as a high school dropout and went on to earn multiple degrees from Penn State; now, I'm pursuing a doctorate at the University of Nebraska. I began as a non-qualifier and went on to become a four-year letter winner and team leader at Penn State University. I started as an undrafted free agent and worked my way through the NFL as a coach and administrator. I once stood in a weight room as a struggling volunteer, and now I've mentored thousands of young men and women. Each chapter of my journey started from humble beginnings, but I've always been committed to finishing strong.

Each milestone whispered the same mandate: **Don't just**

start and finish, but finish on Fire.

That's why my next chapter is clear: move into **athletic administration** so I can equip coaches and student-athletes to finish their own races academically, spiritually, and relationally. I want every player who ever sweated through one of my lifts to believe, *"If Coach Felder could go from 'statistic' to scholar, I can finish strong, too."*

More people watch our lives than we ever speak to, and I'm grateful for that unseen audience. My prayer is that when they watch our marriage, family, and calling, they'll see two truths:

Starting matters.

Finishing matters more.

Spiritual Devotion

"I have fought the good fight, I have finished the race, I have kept the faith."
2 Timothy 4:7

Paul's words capture my heartbeat. Finishing isn't about perfect stats; it's about faithful stewardship. It's keeping the faith when diplomas feel distant, when marriage feels fragile, when dreams feel delayed. **God is the foundation** of every plan, thought, and breath, and because He finishes what He starts, so will we.

The Leadership Lesson

Great leaders are **finishers**:

Commitment: They honor vows on wedding altars, in locker rooms, in classrooms.

Consistency: They show up on the mundane days when applause is absent.

Continuity: They leverage every finish line as someone else's starting line.

If your people see you complete the hard things, they'll believe they can, too.

The Challenge to the Reader

Identify an unfinished assignment, a relationship to mend, a degree to complete, a dream to revive.

Write one next step and schedule it this week.

Pray for finishing grace: *"Lord, help me complete what You entrusted to me on fire, not on fumes."*

Now pray:

> *"Lord God, thank You for every beginning You've given me and for the grace to finish what matters most. I don't want just to get by; I want to finish with fire. Ignite my spirit with boldness, faith, and endurance. Remind me that each test, each delay, and each victory has purpose. Strengthen my commitment to my marriage, my family, and my calling. May my journey inspire others to persevere. And when the whistle blows for my final lap, may I cross the line with joy, knowing I ran my race with fire, faith, and honor. In Jesus' name, Amen."*

Because someday the whistle will blow for all of us. When it does, may we look back with fearless joy and say, **"I finished with fire."**

☩

†

†

SEE YOU ON THE FIELD

Close this book, but don't close the playbook of your life.

Every chapter you've just read was built from real moments: painful losses, powerful wins, quiet nights of doubt, and early mornings of grit. From dropping out of high school in Philly to earning multiple degrees and becoming a coach, mentor, husband, father, and leader, I've lived every lesson in these pages. If there's one truth I want you to remember, it's this:

**The inside game determines
how far the outside game can go.**

You don't have to be perfect to make an impact. I wasn't. I'm still not. I got kicked out of high school. I slept on the floor. I had my truck repossessed. I've been broke, tired, and uncertain. But I never stayed there. I kept showing up with my mind right, with my faith strong, and with a heart set on finishing what I started.

That's the game I want you to play.

**One where character matters
more than clout.**

Where effort beats excuses.

**Where you honor your name
and the people who built you.**

This journey has taken me from North Philly to the NFL, from coaching high school players to guiding young men at Power 5 universities, from being the student in the back of the room to leading programs and shaping lives. And I'm still running my race, working to become an athletic director, build leadership academies, and open doors for those who come from where I came from. But now, I'm handing the ball off to you.

What will you do with your inside game?

Because the truth is, we're all on the clock. One day, the stadium lights go out, the crowd fades, and your name is no longer called over the loudspeaker. What's left? The *legacy*. The *impact*. The *people you poured into*. The moments *when you showed up*, even when it was hard.

So here's my challenge to you: Step onto your field, lead your team, love your people. Write your story with courage and purpose.

And when we meet again, whether on the sidelines, in the locker room, or at a moment when life demands your best, I'll look you in the eye, smile, and say the same thing I've said to thousands of young men.

"Let's go to work."

~Gus "BigDawg" Felder

ACKNOWLEDGMENTS

First, I give thanks to **God**, the author and finisher of every chapter of my life. Without His grace, none of these pages would exist.

Barbara Ann Felder, my mother, your strength, patience, and boundless love shaped four boys and an entire North Philadelphia neighborhood. You were passionate, caring, and enduring through it all. Thank you for your unwavering love and for being a mother not just to your sons, but to so many others. God bless you and rest in heaven.

My brothers, Kendrick, Kevin, and Jamel Felder, thank you for walking with me, pushing me, and honoring the legacy of our parents every day. I love you, and I'm proud to be your brother.

Jim Nuding, my father-in-law, thank you for blessing me with Kelly and for trusting me to lead, love, and protect her. Your trust has meant more than words can express.

Coach John "JT" Thomas, you taught me one of the most valuable lessons of my life: the power of accountability. Thank you for maintaining a high standard and showing me how to live without excuses.

Sally Johnson of Berwick, Pennsylvania, you welcomed me into your home and heart like a son. Your love and support during such a critical time in my life were a turning point I will never forget.

Coach George Curry, you didn't just coach me; you shaped me. You taught me what it means to be a man, how to lead, how to finish, and how to stand tall both on and off the field.

Coach Cosmo Curry, a brother in the weight room and in life, thank you for being a mentor, a motivator, and a friend through every season of growth.

Pastor Thomas Settles, your wisdom, friendship, and prophetic insight have helped keep me grounded in the Word. You reminded me that I may be the only Bible some people will ever read, and I carry that truth with reverence and a sense of responsibility.

Coach Randy Chambers, a spiritual brother and leader whose impact reaches far beyond the field, thank you for your prayers, your example, and your relentless faith in me and God's purpose for my life.

To the many players, coaches, teammates, and mentors who helped shape my journey, **thank you.** There are too many names to list, but your fingerprints are on every page of this book.

And finally, to **my wife, Kelly,** and our children **Destiny, Jazmin, Alexa, EJ,** and **Faith,** you are my heart, my legacy, and the reason I keep pressing forward. You've given me the most excellent titles I'll ever hold: husband, father, and leader of our home. I love you beyond words.

With deep gratitude and love,

—Gus "BigDawg" Felder

ABOUT THE AUTHOR

Gus "BigDawg" Felder is a husband, father, mentor, coach, and leader with a mission rooted in faith, perseverance, and purpose. Born and raised in the Strawberry Mansion section of North Philadelphia, Gus transformed from a high school dropout into a college graduate, earning several degrees from Penn State University, where he also played as a key member on the offensive line under legendary coach Joe Paterno.

After a brief stint in the NFL with the Cleveland Browns, Gus transitioned into coaching and leadership development, taking on roles in high schools, HBCUs, major NCAA programs, and the NFL, including the University of Georgia, Clark Atlanta University, the University of Miami, and the Carolina Panthers. He currently serves as the Executive Director of Player Development at the University of Nebraska.

With over two decades of experience mentoring young people through athletics, Gus's calling extends beyond the weight room and football field. He is a passionate speaker, spiritual leader, and community builder focused on helping student-athletes grow holistically, mind, body, and spirit.

Gus is married to his high school sweetheart, Kelly, and together they've raised five children and two grandchildren, modeling love, endurance, and the power of finishing what you start. The Inside Game is his first book, a reflection of the lessons that shaped his life and the blueprint he hopes will inspire the next generation to lead with purpose, faith, and grit.

†

†

†

†

†

†

www.ingramcontent.com/pod-product-compliance
Lightning Source LLC
Chambersburg PA
CBHW060201050426
42446CB00013B/2927